Visit us at
www.adventuresofscubajack.com
for more FUN Learning!

Beneath the waves where the sunlight plays,
A young boy snorkels on bright blue days.
His name is Finn, with a curious grin,
Exploring the ocean, where wonders begin.

He greets a turtle, so wise and slow,
"Hello there, friend! Where do you go?"
The turtle replies, with a smile so wide,
"I'm off to a reef, would you like a ride?"

Finn dives deeper, where colors abound,
Fish of all shapes are swimming around.
A seahorse waved with a flick of its tail,
"Join our parade on the ocean trail!"

Finn couldn't resist the seahorse's call,
He swam to the reef, feeling quite small.
But size didn't matter; the creatures were kind,
In this underwater world, treasures he'd find.

A dolphin appeared with a cheerful squeak,
"Race me, Finn, to that coral peak!"
With a laugh, Finn swam as fast as he could,
But the dolphin sped past—he knew that it would!

An octopus waved with eight wiggly arms,
"I'll show you my tricks and all of my charms!"
It spun in a circle, a dance of delight,
Then vanished in ink—a magical sight.

A crab on the sand, with claws that clicked,
Said, "Careful, my friend, these rocks are slick!"
Finn thanked the crab with a grateful cheer,
"Your kindness is clear, it's lovely down here!"

Then a whale sang low, a melody deep,
Calling the creatures from their coral keep.
"Join us, dear Finn, in the ocean's song,
For here in the sea, you've belonged all along."

Together they sang, a harmonious tune,
Under the glow of the silvery moon.
Finn marveled at how the ocean could bring,
Friendship and joy in everything.

When the day grew late and the tide pulled away,
Finn waved goodbye to the friends of the bay.
"I'll visit again, I promise you this,
The ocean's my home, a place of pure bliss."

How many sea turtles do you see? [3] [2] [1]

How many Sea horses do you see? [4] [1] [3]

How many Angel Fish do you see?   5   3   4

Fun Fact:

One of the biggest predatory fish on Earth, great white sharks may reach lengths of 20 feet and weigh more than 5,000 pounds.

Trace the Word

Great White Shark

Great White Shark

Great White Shark

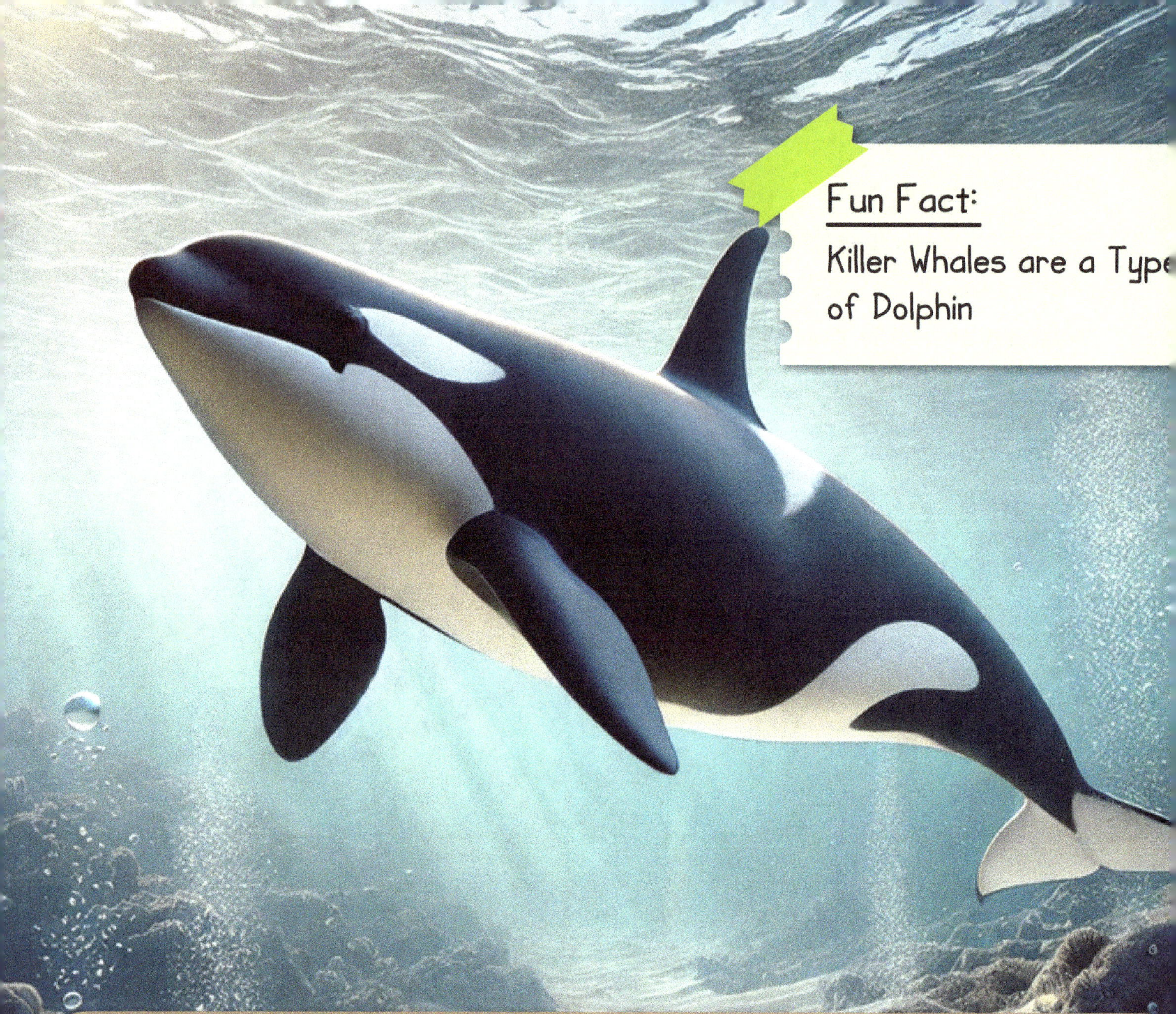

Fun Fact:

Killer Whales are a Type of Dolphin

Trace the Word

Orca Orca Orca

Orca Orca Orca

Orca Orca Orca

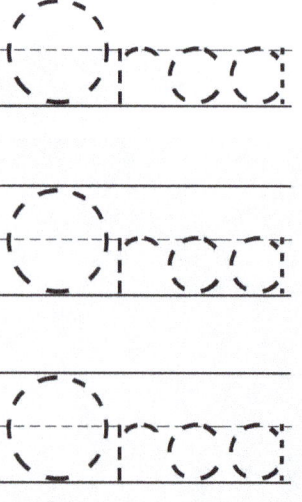

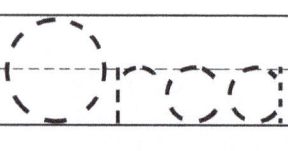

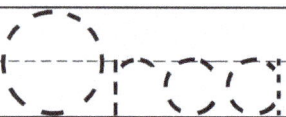

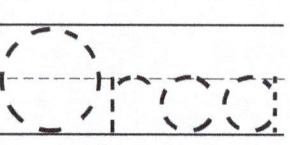

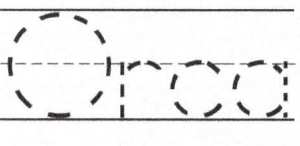

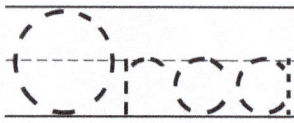

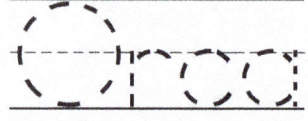

Fun Fact:

There are Over 2000 Species of Jellyfish

Trace the Word

Jelly Fish Jelly Fish

Jelly Fish Jelly Fish

Jelly Fish Jelly Fish

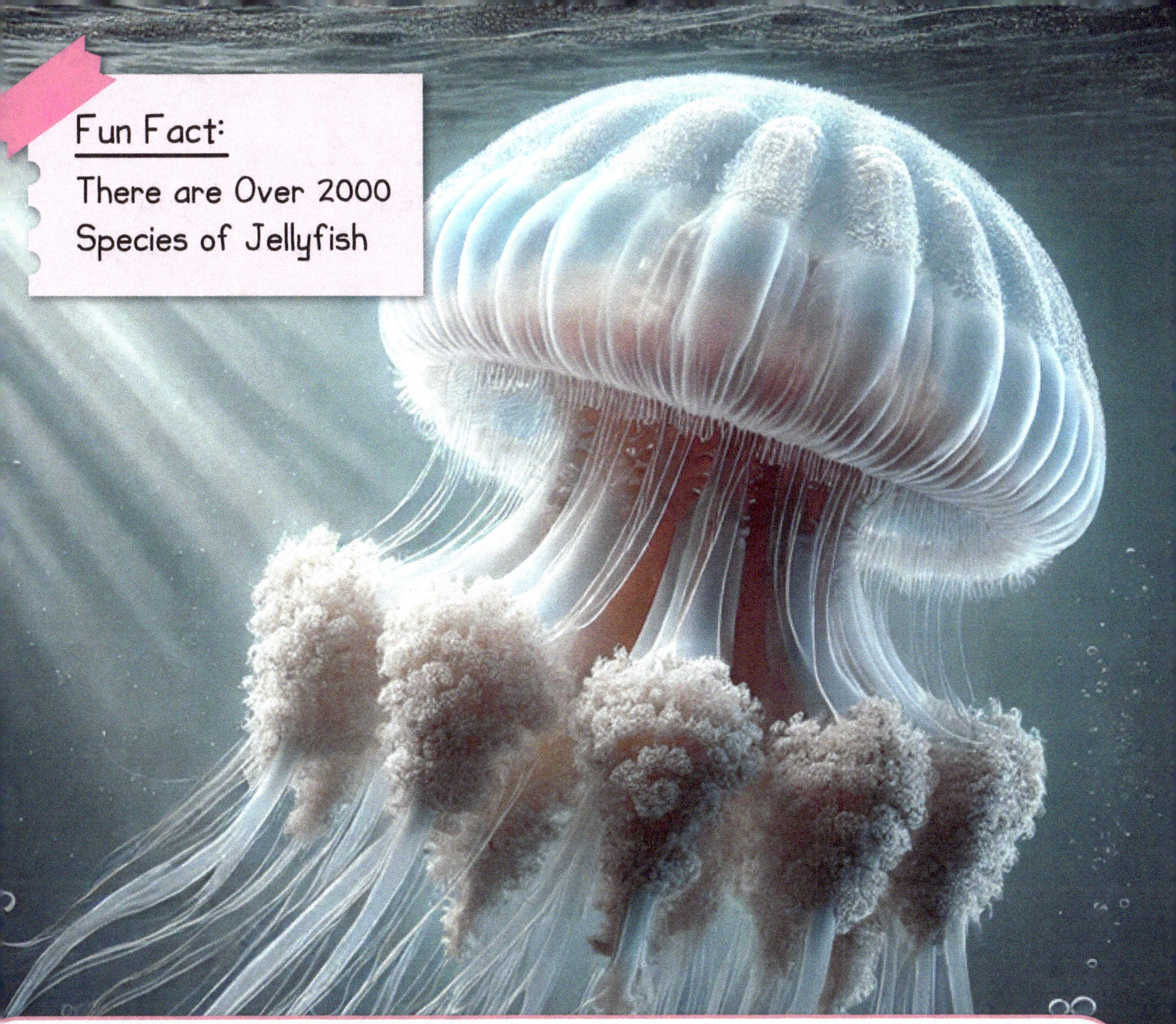

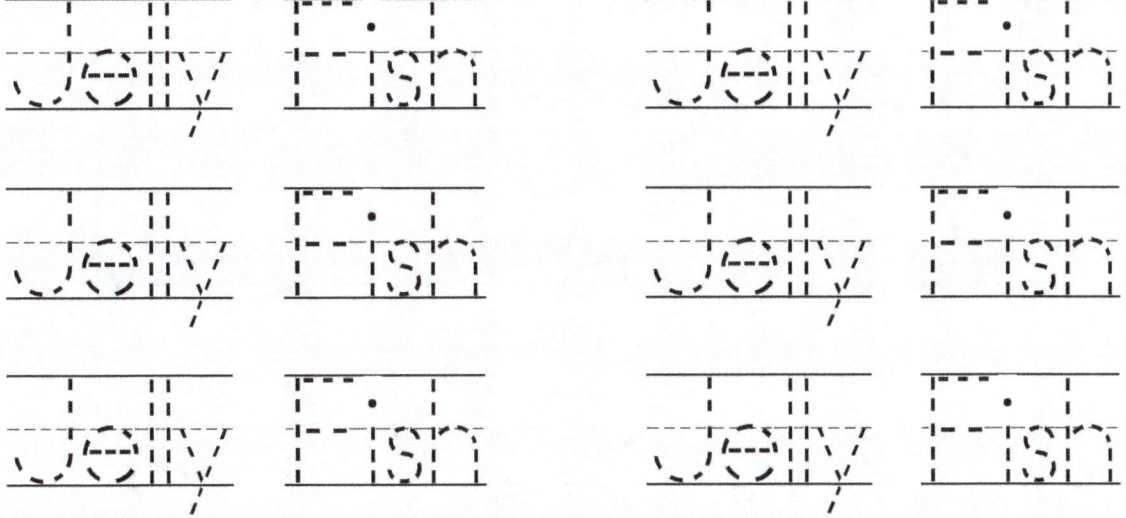

Fun Fact:
Seals can live in both polar and tropical waters.

Trace the Word

Seal Seal Seal
Seal Seal Seal
Seal Seal Seal

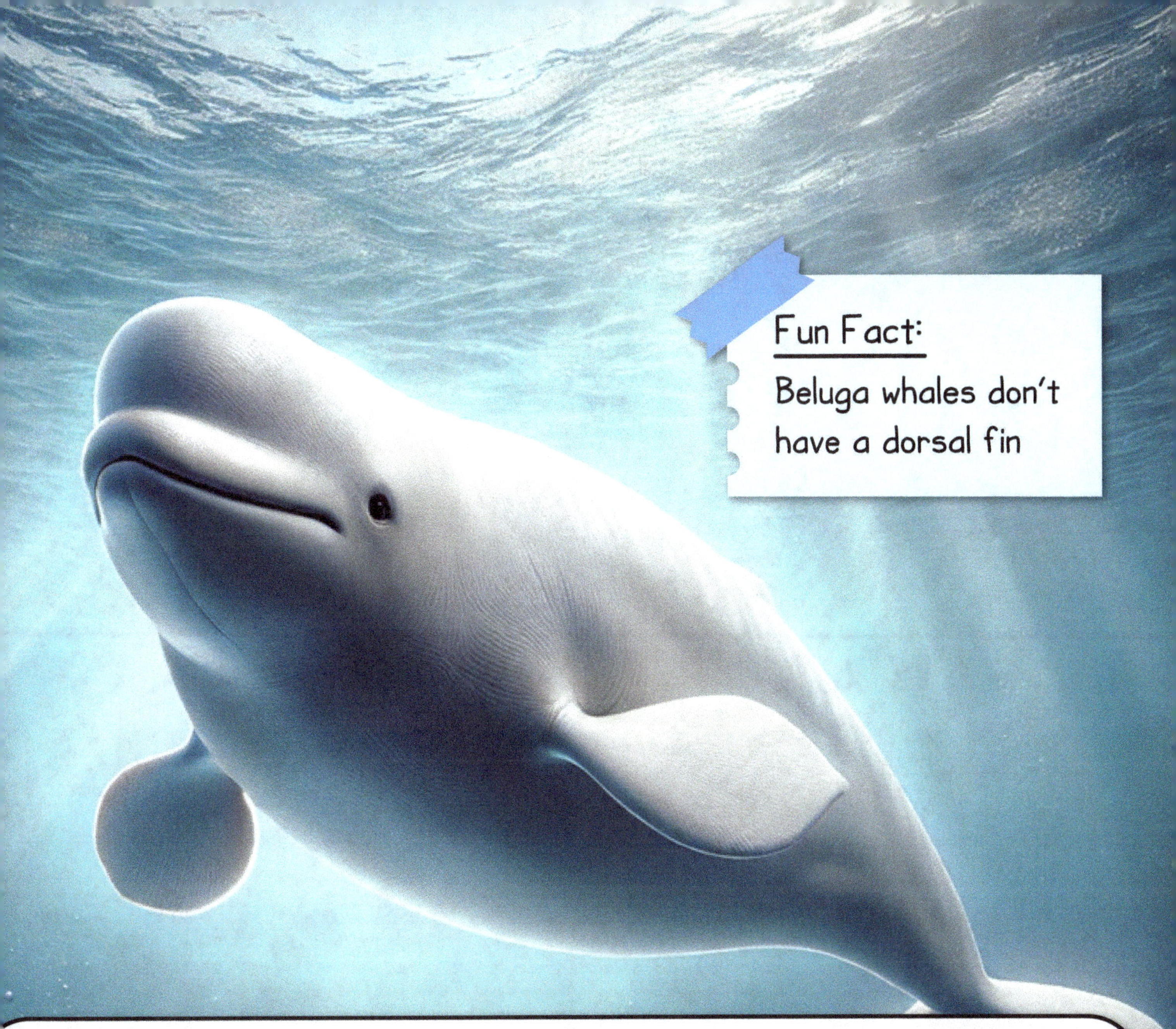

Fun Fact:

Beluga whales don't have a dorsal fin

Trace the Word

Beluga	Beluga	Beluga
Beluga	Beluga	Beluga
Beluga	Beluga	Beluga

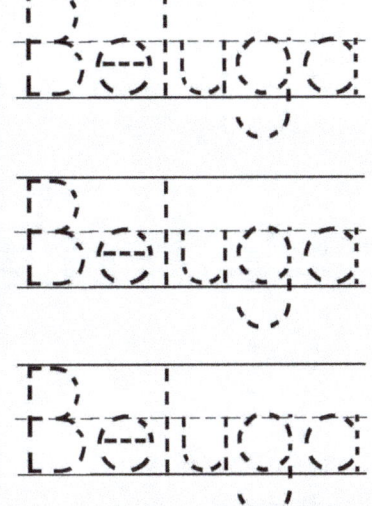

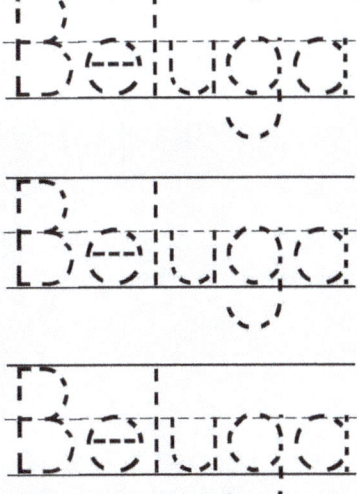

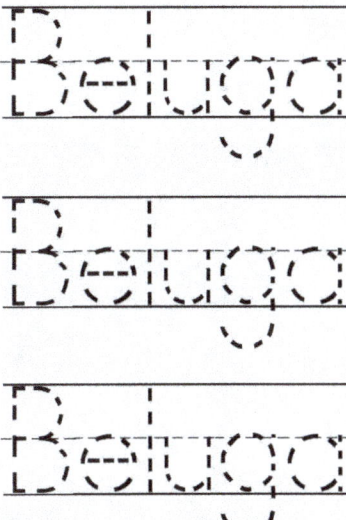

Fun Fact:
Lionfish have venomous spines

Trace the Word

Lion Fish   Lion Fish

Lion Fish   Lion Fish

Lion Fish   Lion Fish

Fun Fact:

Black tip sharks often appear in shallow coastal waters that are only 12 inches deep.

Trace the Word

Black Tip Shark

Black Tip Shark

Black Tip Shark

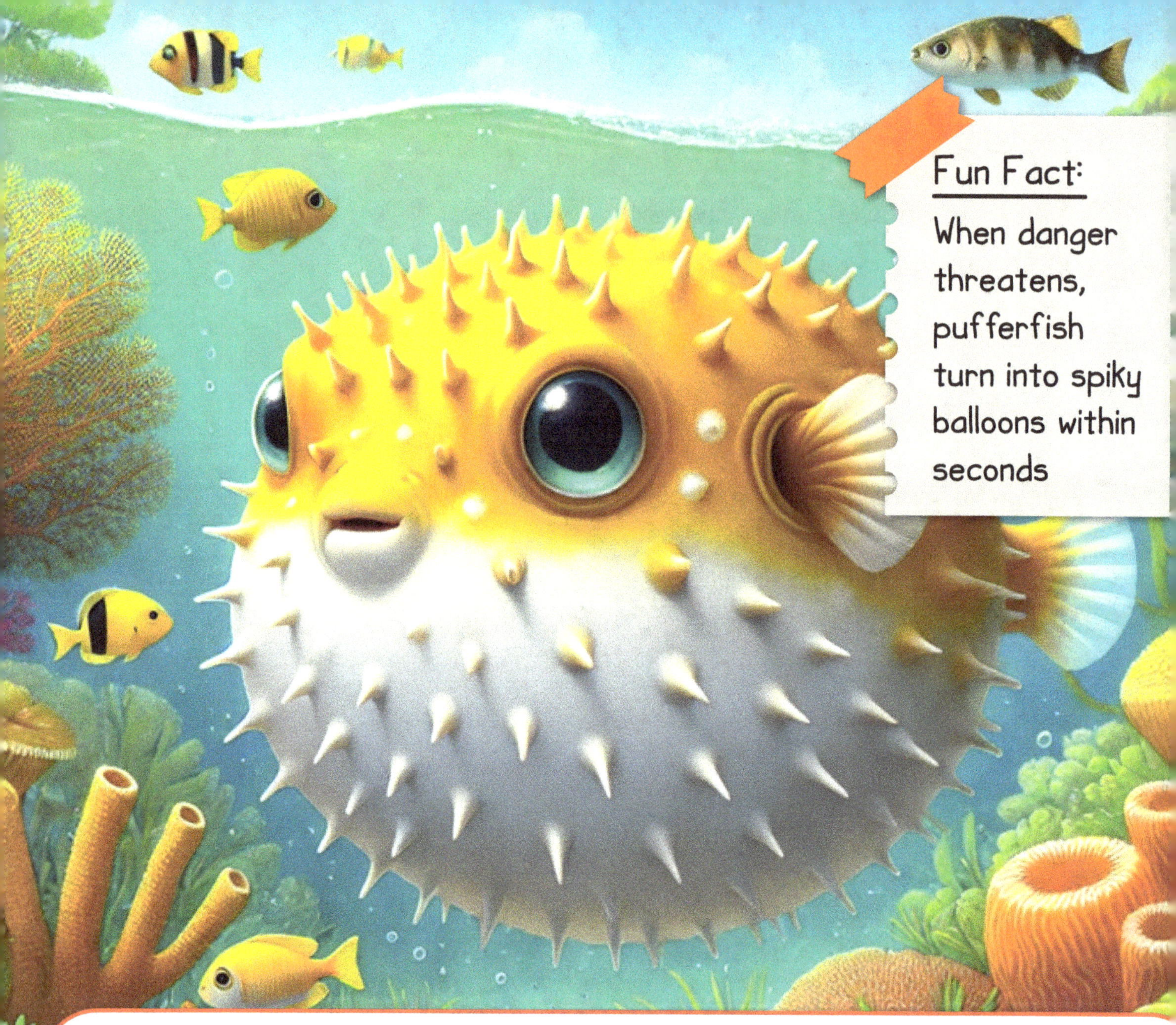

Fun Fact:

When danger threatens, pufferfish turn into spiky balloons within seconds

Trace the Word

Puffer Fish Puffer Fish

Puffer Fish Puffer Fish

Puffer Fish Puffer Fish

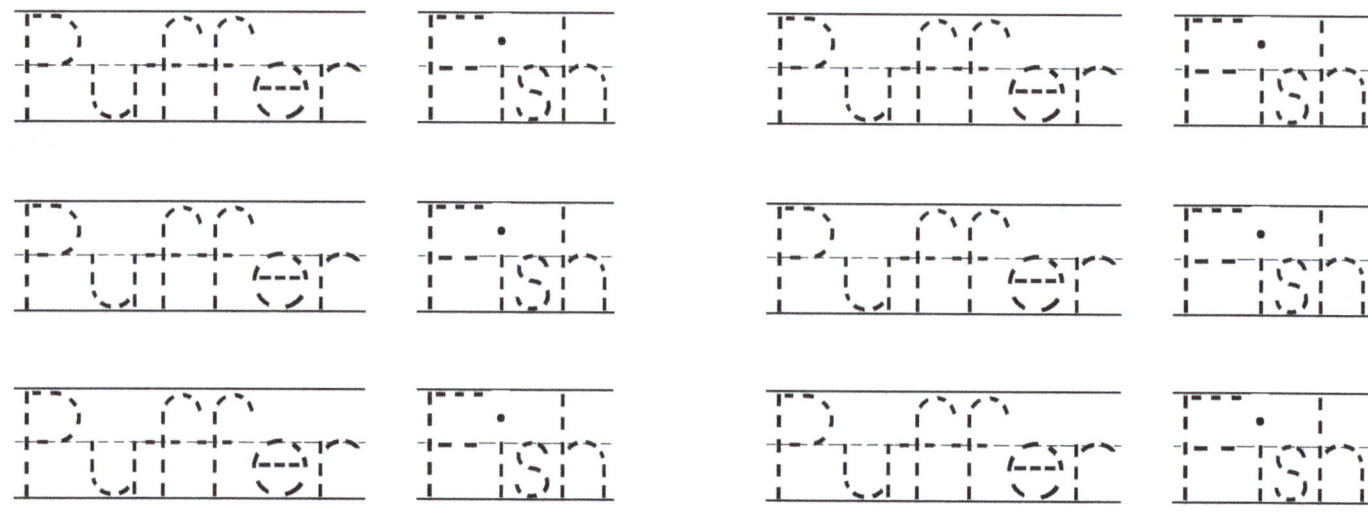

Fun Fact:
The Blue Whale is the Largest Animal on Earth Weighing up to 200 Tons

Trace the Word

Blue Whale   Blue Whale
Blue Whale   Blue Whale
Blue Whale   Blue Whale

Fun Fact:

Sea Otters Hold Hands When Sleeping to Keep from Drifting Apart

Trace the Word

Sea Otter Sea Otter

Sea Otter Sea Otter

Sea Otter Sea Otter

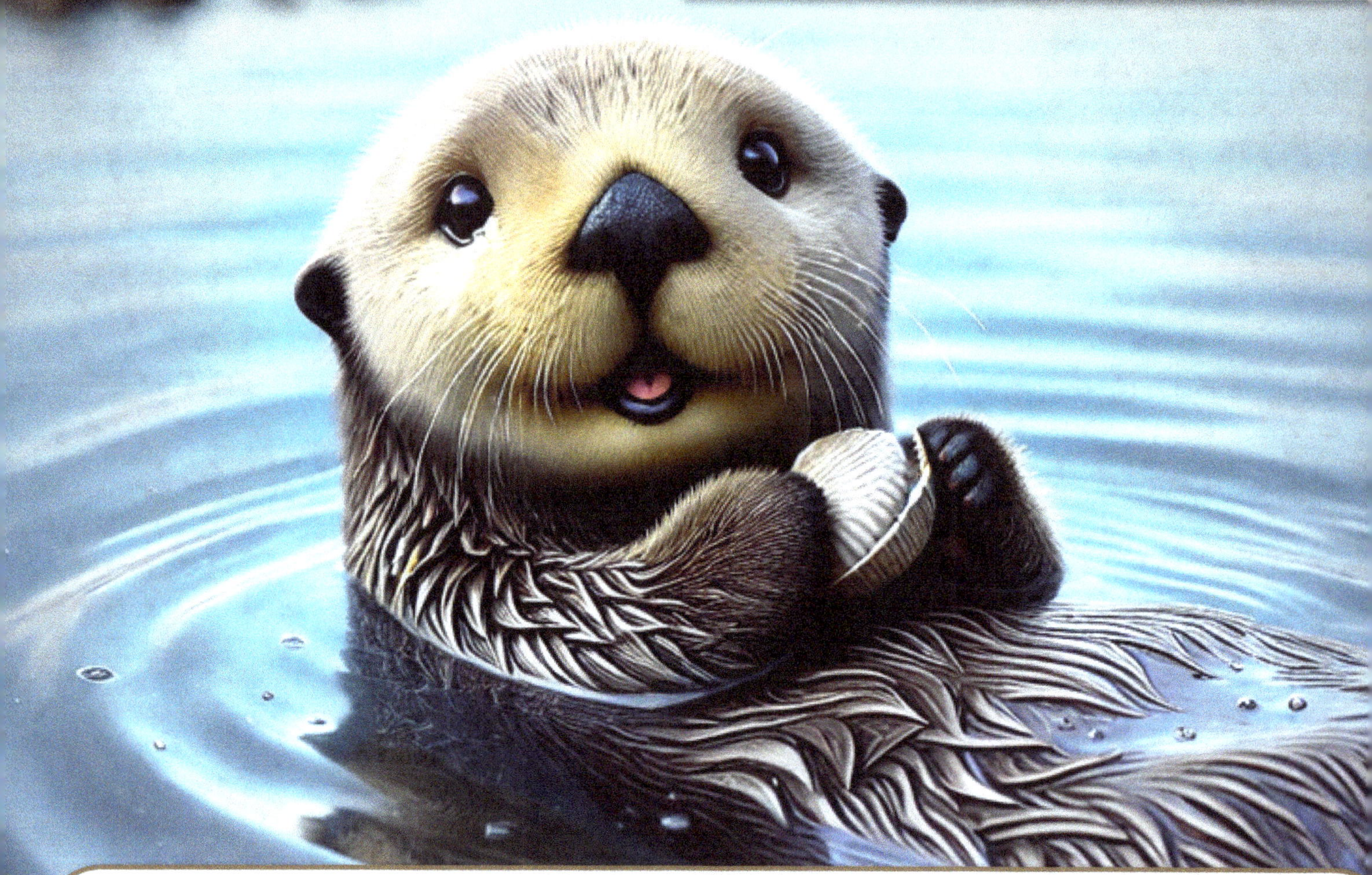

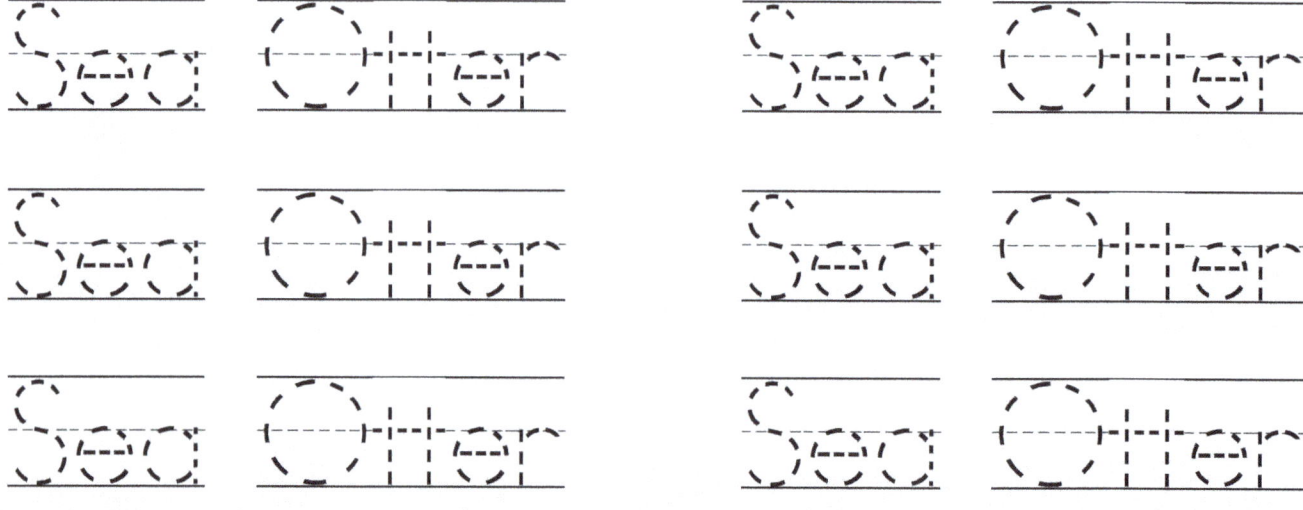

www.ingramcontent.com/pod-product-compliance
Lightning Source LLC
LaVergne TN
LVHW060134080526
838201LV00118B/3051